Fam ous
ROCKS

by Anne Mansk

HOUGHTON MIFFLIN   BOSTON

Famous Granite Rocks

Some rocks stand out from others. Special qualities make these rocks famous.

The pilgrims landed near Plymouth Rock in 1620. Plymouth Rock is made of granite. Granite is an igneous rock. An igneous rock is heated inside the earth. It melts. Then it hardens as it rises to the Earth's crust.

Plymouth Rock is visited by nearly one million people each year.

Independence Rock in Wyoming was a welcome sight for pioneers.

Another famous rock made of granite is Independence Rock. In the 1800's, many people moved west. They came in wagons pulled by horses. The trip was hard. They hoped to reach the famous rock on the trail by the Fourth of July. Then they knew that their trip was on schedule.

Men, women, and children were happy to see this huge rock. They could rest for a while. Many of them wrote their names on the rock. Then others who came after them would know they were safe.

Mount Rushmore is in South Dakota.

This large piece of granite is actually the side of a mountain. It has the faces of famous people carved into it. The heads of four Presidents are on Mount Rushmore. Workers used dynamite to shape parts of the hard rock. It was dangerous work.

The wind and weather slowly wear away the surface of the granite. This is called weathering. Over the years, the faces will look smoother. Some of the details will be worn away.

A Colorful Rock

Picture yourself walking in the hot desert. You look up and see a large oval shape. It rises a thousand feet in the air. It is over two miles long. Where are you? You are in Australia looking at Ayer's Rock, also known as Uluru.

Ayer's Rock is sedimentary rock. Sedimentary rock is a type of rock made up of Earth materials like clay or sand. The sediments in Ayer's Rock are sand. This type of rock is called sandstone. Ayer's Rock seems to change color during the day. The rays of the sun shine on the different colored sand sediments.

Ayer's Rock is in the Australian desert.

Mysterious Rocks

Some rocks are mysterious. Scientists understand what type of rocks they are. But they wonder about how people were able to move them.

Stonehenge is a circle of large heavy stones. Many of the stones are almost 30 feet high. Each one weighs around 50 tons. Stonehenge dates back 5,000 years. How were people able to carry and lift these stones into position?

Stonehenge in Salisbury Plain, England

Stone figures on Easter Island

These stone figures are also mysterious. They are found on Easter Island. The island was formed by a volcano. It is thousands of miles away from land. On it are over 600 huge statues. Each one was carved from a block of soft stone from a volcano.

Some of these stone "guards" weigh up to 80 tons. The craftsmen used cutting tools made out of hard volcanic rock. First they chipped the statue out of the rock wall. Then they had to move the statue up to 14 miles away. The size and weight of these rocks would make this a hard job for anyone.

**Part of the Giant's Causeway
extends into the sea.**

A Road of Rocks

Are these rocks part of the moon? No, they are called the Giant's Causeway. A causeway is a road. Thousands of stone columns look like steps that lead to the sea. There is an Irish story that says this rock road was built by giants. They needed a road to take them to an island.

The Giant's Causeway was formed by lava. The lava flowed to the sea. Each time it cooled, new columns were formed. The rocks in the Giant's Causeway are basalt. Basalt is an igneous rock just like the granite found at Mount Rushmore.